A labor of love applying extraoı             , ————···
Gray's *Salient* sharpens the details of the record, even while broadening the record's range.

Taking as her occasion the Battle of Ypres in World War I (and, in a signature move, introducing elements of Tantric figuration into the textual design), Gray interweaves analytic and lyric threads—microcosm with macrocosm, explication with implication, scholarship with song.

The patterns cross conventional lines—time lines, gender lines, genre lines, lines of authority. Earth in the body, language in the jaw-hinge, spirit in the air—they all occasion insight. Where female forces make their metaphysics felt, they serve as metonymies for the poet's sensibility in warlord territories.

And that particular form of selflessness by which an author enters another's characteristic world of circumstance is enlisted as part of an epistemological enterprise: not only are the objects and events of history inquired into, but also the particulars of the inquirer's life a hundred years later, and the timeless nature of the act of inquiry itself.

Through fractal patterns in the zoom, and faithful groundwork in the moment, Gray achieves her evanescent figures: man in motion, motion in a man; hand out of time, time out of hand. As wise to the seductions of private betrayal as to those of common faith, the poet makes her links and leaps between the counterparts, instead of building battlements. In driest wit, intelligence can shine. For linguists, "now" is, after all, a slider.

And every word's a stab at faith. Our meanings always have to leap a gap. We go about divining with a bloody eye; we go about our beatings with a blinded heart. We stand on hind legs with our forepaws raised: what's salient is sometimes what is pointing outwards. In many moving ways, we aim to get our bearings on our dyings.

But Gray concludes this striking work by praying that the goddesses will do what humans never could: Just stay.

—HEATHER MᶜHUGH

# SALIENT

## ALSO BY ELIZABETH T. GRAY, JR.

*Poetry*
Series | India (2015)

*Translations*
Wine & Prayer: Eighty Ghazals from the Diwan of Hafiz (2019)
Iran: Poems of Dissent (2013)
The Green Sea of Heaven: Fifty Ghazals from the Diwan of Hafiz (1995)

Elizabeth T. Gray, Jr.

# SALIENT

A POEM

*with an afterword by Nathaniel Tarn*

A NEW DIRECTIONS
PAPERBOOK ORIGINAL

Manufactured in the United States of America
New Directions Books are printed on acid-free paper
First published as a New Directions Paperbook (NDP1481) in 2020
Design by Erik Rieselbach

*Library of Congress Cataloging-in-Publication Data*
Names: Gray, Jr., Elizabeth T., 1952– author.
Title: Salient : a poem / Elizabeth T. Gray, Jr. ; with an afterword
by Nathaniel Tarn
Description: New York : New Directions Publishing, 2020.
Identifiers: LCCN 2020003272 | ISBN 9780811229241 (paperback :
acid-free paper) | ISBN 9780811229258 (ebook)
Subjects: LCGFT: Poetry.
Classification: LCC PS3607.R3889 S25 2020 | DDC 811/.6—dc23
LC record available at https://lccn.loc.gov/2020003272

10 9 8 7 6 5 4 3 2 1

New Directions Books are published for James Laughlin
by New Directions Publishing Corporation
80 Eighth Avenue, New York 10011

*For John Peck,*
*Matthew T. Kapstein,*
*the Lady in the Café,*
*the Patricia's,*
*and*
*the Infantry Captain with the Cat—*


*my guides to the ground.*

# CONTENTS

# PREFACE

This work began by juxtaposing two obsessions of mine that took root in the late 1960s: (1) the Battle of Passchendaele, fought by the British Army in Belgian Flanders in late 1917, and (2) the *chöd* ritual, the core "severance" practice of a lineage founded by Machik Lapdrön, the great twelfth-century female Tibetan Buddhist saint.

I have no complete explanation as to why these two subjects have remained of abiding interest to me, but I can tell you a bit about each of them.

## Passchendaele

In the fall of 1968, assigned to write a paper for my high school Modern European History class, I went to the school library where I came upon a bound set of *The Illustrated London News* for the years 1914–1918. Aware that (like our own *Life* magazine) pictures would dominate, it seemed an easy way to cruise the era for a topic.

The issues from late 1917 that covered the Third Battle of Ypres—a great, glorious, and decisive victory of the British against the Germans and all odds—offered dark drawings of the battlefield, of teams of exhausted men working enormous artillery pieces, of lines of courageous soldiers moving across difficult ground toward ultimate victory. Rich fodder for an easy essay.

A brief review of secondary sources revealed the *News*'s coverage to be, shall we say, incomplete. While to this day historians argue about the decisions made by the generals and politicians, the Battle of Passchendaele remains unimaginable and the poster child for the horrors of the Great War: waves of exhausted men advancing slowly uphill for weeks in relentless rain through waist-deep mud into artillery and machine-gun fire in order to capture a few yards of strategically insignificant ground. There were roughly 500,000 German and Allied casualties. Almost 90,000 British and Commonwealth soldiers who fought in the Ypres Salient vanished there and have no known grave. And this bit of ground was only a small segment of the Western Front.

These scenes felt shockingly familiar (how could that be? who was there?) but unfathomable. Was this victory? Who could have called it that? Why? What kind of officers would give such orders? What kind of men would follow them? What kind of courage enabled them to walk into mud, into walls of shellfire, into machine guns? For so far? For so long? In the rain? How could one imagine this? How did one explain it to oneself, to loved ones? Who were these men? How do we grasp them? Where are they?

In the decades that followed I continued to collect material related to those weeks in late October and early November 1917. I read not only history, poetry, and fiction, but also unit diaries; contemporary reports and individual accounts; survey information and maps of all kinds; treatises on aerial photography and artillery tactics; and manuals on field engineering and tactical planning. I walked the ground, between and behind the lines, campaign maps in hand, for weeks at a time, in all seasons and all weathers.

*Protective Magic*

I grew up with terrible nightmares, and across from our town's seventeenth-century burial ground. I have always been deeply interested in protective magic.

For me, the late 1960s were infused with Eastern religions. During the autumn in which I discovered the war in Flanders I also discovered W. Y. Evans-Wentz's translations of *The Tibetan Book of the Dead* and of texts on Tibetan yogic practices, including the *chöd* rite. As I understood it at the time, the *chöd* rite required you to seek out a haunted place—a charnel ground, cemetery, or desolate place—and, once there, to visualize dismembering your own body and offering the pieces thereof, as food, to all the demons and other beings that seek to harm you. Once sated, they would vanish, and you would be safe. Forever. Here were my wrathful deities who, somehow, could be transformed into teachers and guardians.

In the decades since, I have worked with Tibetan scholars, spent considerable time in the Himalaya, and met many of the hundreds of translators who have made a wide variety of Tibetan sacred and secular works available in English. Biographies of Machik Lapdrön, *chöd*-related texts, doctrinal works from the various lineages, and studies of the wrathful pantheon and protective magic (Buddhist and Bön) are now widely available. I understand more clearly now that the practice that had fascinated me was about severing one's attachment to one's individual self, and in an act of absolute compassion making, in dismemberment, what the military often refers to as "the ultimate sacrifice."

I began *Salient* by placing these two poles of obsession in proximity to one another. And waiting. In the charged field between them I originally thought I might find The Missing. And that they, too, might finally be safe.

I am grateful to those, living and dead, who have proved good companions on confusing ground. The misunderstandings are mine. May the protectors be patient.

IEPER/YPRES, BELGIUM
NOVEMBER 2017

# SALIENT

**salient,** *a.* and *n.*

## A. *adj.*

1. a. Leaping, jumping; *esp.* of animals.
   b. Of water: Jetting forth; leaping upwards.
   c. Of the pulse: Beating strongly. *poet.*

2. (*Heraldry.*) Having the hind legs in sinister base and the forepaws elevated near together in the dexter chief, as if in the act of leaping.

3. In old medical use, the heart as it first appears in an embryo; hence, the first beginning of life or motion; the starting-point of anything.

4. Of an angle: Pointing outward, as an ordinary angle of a polygon (opposed to *re-entrant*); chiefly in *Fortification*.

5. a. Of material things: Standing above or beyond the general surface or outline; jutting out; prominent among a number of objects.
   b. Of immaterial things, qualities, etc.: Standing out from the rest; prominent, conspicuous; often in phrase "salient point." Also *Psychol.*, standing out or prominent in consciousness.

## B. *n. Fortif.*

1. A salient angle or part of a work.

2. A narrow projection or spur of land extending from a larger feature; a spur-like area of land, esp. one held by a line of offence or defence, as in trench-warfare;

   *spec.* (frequently with *the* and capital initial) that at Ypres in western Belgium, the scene of severe fighting in the war of 1914–1918.

   —from the *Oxford English Dictionary* (2004)

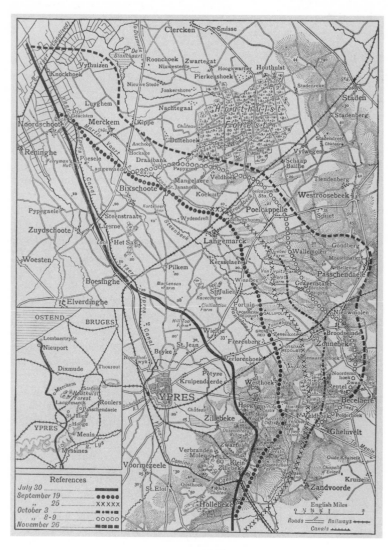

*The Ypres Salient*
*The British Advance, 30 July to 26 November 1917*

"This volume contains the account of the two Flanders offensives of 1917 called, officially, 'The Battle of Messines 1917' (7th–14th June), and 'The Battles of Ypres 1917' (31st July–10th November)—the latter better known as 'Third Ypres' or even 'Passchendaele.' The Ypres offensive, according to the official 'Battle Nomenclature,' includes eight battles: Pilkem Ridge (31st July–2nd August), Langemarck (16th–18th August), Menin Road Ridge (20th–25th September), Polygon Wood (26th September–3rd October), Broodseinde (4th October), Poelcappelle (9th October), First Passchendaele (12th October) and Second Passchendaele (26th October–10th November)."

—Brigadier-General Sir James E. Edmonds, C.B., C.M.G., Ed. *History of the Great War: Military Operations: France and Belgium, 1917. Vol. II, 7th June–10th November: Messines and Third Ypres (Passchendaele).* (London: Her Majesty's Stationery Office, 1948. iii.)


*"Although the past is still clear in your mind, listen well and I will pretend to explain it."*

—The Goddess Tārā to Machik Labdrön, 11–12c. Tibetan female saint and founder of the *Chöd* lineage of Tantric Buddhism. Machik Labdrön, *Machik's Complete Explanation: Clarifying the Meaning of Chöd.* Translated by Sarah Harding. (Ithaca, New York, and Boulder, Colorado: Snow Lion Publications, Tsadra Foundation, 2003. 87.)

Scaled up to the level of war magic, the violent repelling rites of the *tantras* became The Big Push, The Big Show, or a Schlieffen Plan.

Large numbers of ritual experts would assemble for performances that could last several days, if not weeks.

The requisite expert officiants and necessary materials had to be assembled and elaborate shrines constructed.

Legions of effigies (*ling ga*) of enemy soldiers would be fashioned from barley flour, butter, and paper, often accompanied by thousands more effigies of the enemy's horses, so that the practitioners in effect re-created the battlefield within the confines of a ritual space.

Thus the resources required for a serious repelling rite were considerable.

455 tons of ammonal for the nineteen mines at Messines, for example, and 33 million shells.

In the last half of the female fire snake year of 1917 it was said that a great number of enemy were coming.

All the farmers and nomads were terrified.

Fifty divisions took part in the ritual performances, and in early November the signs emerged.

A great snowstorm fell.

After that, a gale rose up, and shreds of cloth, like prayer flags, froze in the craters.

They were buried beneath the snow, men along with their horses and pack animals.

Not even one escaped death.

When the snow melted, the Lower Hor-pa and Ser-myog came down out of the mountains and when they were done stripping the bodies there was nothing there.

TAKING REFUGE
The Playing of "Last Post"
Menin Gate Memorial to the Missing, Ypres
Every evening at 8:00 p.m.


Pick up your instrument.
Place it to your lips.

When you play the first notes visualize
that from here to the heights of the circled hills
The Missing
can hear and that when the notes reach them
they stop what they are doing,
come to attention, and turn
toward the sound.

Make the next notes hang in the air.
Make them say "Gather here!"

Imagine that the men hear this, that they emerge,
eagerly, from their individual places
and begin to remember themselves.

When you blow the last notes they come,
with great urgency, all of them.

Visualize them assembled
in the fields before you and imagine
that they inhabit for a moment
this song.

"To the War Pilgrim, arriving at Ypres with mind steeped in the remembrance of endurance and suffering, that arrival must come with a curious shock.

We picture the Ypres of war—ruin—desolation—emptiness. We step from the train to a brightly new and very complete town. We make our way through streets to the central Place, and [find] here a square of hotels, shops, houses . . .

There is merit in this newness, in that it has followed the old lines, and as far as possible has reproduced the style of the old town, and we are lost in admiration of the industry of this people, already housed, and—after the four years' nightmare, beginning life afresh. But it is all very disconcerting for the Pilgrim!"

—Lieut.-General Sir William Pulteney and Beatrix Brice, *The Immortal Salient: An Historical Record and Complete Guide for Pilgrims to Ypres*. (London: The Ypres League, John Murray, 1925. 20.)

## LOOKING FOR THE WAR

Crest Farm was never called that
on German maps; was not
actually a farm; was captured at great cost
by 72nd Battalion, 4th Canadian Division
(Seaforth Highlanders, Vancouver)
on 30th October 1917; was
the jumping-off line for 27th Battalion,
2nd Canadian Division (City of Winnipeg)
at 0600 on 6th November but is
not here—no signs
of it or what happened,
just a small car park, pub, this circle
of maples, a bakery, this line
of tidy houses down a road.

## IN SOME WAYS THE SITUATION IS ANALOGOUS TO THAT FACING SECOND ARMY IN 1915

The trig and mapping situation is complex. Here I am straddling the Franco-Belgian frontier and several different sets of trig data (of varying antiquity) exist for the region.

The trigonometric problem is that although others have begun to use the Belgian spheroid, origin, azimuth, and sheetlines as the basis for their own survey (referring the French data to these), the absence of central geodetic control at some GHQ leaves each of us to our own devices.

My situation is difficult: I have to reconcile the trig and leveling data of the various systems available for this area (including the French admiralty triangulation and British cross-Channel work) with my own emotions—complex mathematical calculations and a feeling of loss.

"He is not missing. He is here."

—Field Marshal Lord Herbert Plumer.
Inauguration of the Menin Gate Memorial to the Missing,
Ypres, Belgium, 24 July 1927

## RECALLING THE *BLA*

The *bla*, "soul," can also leave the body as a result of a frightening event or unbearable pain. In such cases, it may be recalled or ordered back by means of a ritual. The *bla* may dwell, temporarily at least, in various places outside the body without risk of any danger. Hence the expression *blas gnas*, "dwelling of the soul," a place where the *bla* takes up residence. It can be a rock or tree, a pond, a small canal or piece of church.

# THE MISSING

It was a test. She asked, *Are they here or not?*
Because the land is flat it is hard to see.

The men may be hidden in that empty space.
The canal was a serious obstacle.

The banks of the dykes are bordered with willows.
The lyric moment at its best.

At the edge of each moment I thought I saw movement.
It was a test. She asked, *Are they here or not?*

The lines kept changing but not by much.
Because the land was flat it was hard to see.

The men may be hidden in that empty space.
The banks of the dykes are bordered with willows.

*You can read this*, she said.
The lines ran right through this cornfield.

Corroded buttons, cap badges, numbered disks.
At the edge of each moment I thought I saw movement.

When the sun came out I was surprised.
I asked, Should I just go home?

The canal was a serious obstacle.
The lyric moment at its best.

The lines kept changing, but not by much.
It was a test. She asked, *Are they here or not?*

Gently, metal on metal. Something on its own terms.
When the sun came out I was surprised.

The lines ran right through this cornfield.
The banks of the dykes are bordered with willows.

The canal was a serious obstacle.
*You can read this*, she said.

## INDIRECT FIRE: SHOOTING FROM THE MAP
## (FROM APPENDIX B)

3.0  Fire is brought to bear on the desired object either by means of direct observation, or by the map.

    3.1  Obviously, what I am looking for can no longer be observed directly. Thus these maps.

4.0  There are difficulties inherent in using a map.

    4.1  Sometimes maps are inaccurate.

        4.1.1  For example, this was the incorrect location of a farm that was no longer there.

    4.2  Your exact position on the map must be known.

5.0  If you know where you are, orient yourself by aligning on some distant, visible point.

    5.1  Assuming I was here now, distant and visible remains a problem.

        5.1.1  Where the Cloth Hall Tower had been, from where the German observation post no longer is, was pretty straightforward.

        5.1.2  Likewise the overpass and on-ramp on the recent extension of the A19.

    5.2  This may be camouflage: the fact that some points are concealed remains concealed.

6.0  If you know where you are but no points are visible, orient yourself by compass. This can be done quite accurately if the error of the compass is known, and this is best ascertained by taking a bearing on the North Star at a time when the pointers of the Great Bear are directly above or below it.

6.1 Stars. Orientation. Alignment. Error.

6.2 Let's say you know where you are. The compass may be useful but it comes to you with an error. Like us every compass bears with it its error.

    6.2.1 The amount of error depends on where it is.

    6.2.2 To find its error in a given location you must measure the divergence between what pulls you and the true, and then

    6.2.3 as the sailors do, you can find your way by the stars or by your instrument with its now familiar error.

6.3 From where you are, a bearing may be taken, at the proper moment, on the North Star and the Bear. But you have to wait.

6.4 Only when the Bear and the Pole align, distant and visible, can you find your instrument's error.

## GENERAL DESCRIPTION OF THE LINE

The first line generally consists of two parts, one an obstacle,
and is continuous except for narrow inconspicuous passages
that may serve as exits.

The supporting line should always be constructed
as a second line in the event that the first line is lost.
It may or may not be continuous—it is preferable that it should be.

There will be a certain number of points
the loss of which would seriously endanger the lines.
These must be carefully concealed for maximum effect,
and should be protected by an obstacle
which may consist of a line.

As to their number or relative position with regard to the first line,
subsequent lines should be constructed so that
the whole of the first line
can be swept with machine gun fire.

## BEAR IN MIND
Trench map sheet 20 SW 4 Bixschoote U.21.c.4.6


Bear in mind
that the contours on this map are incorrect.
The river's meander as shown
just north of Ruisseau and Signal Farms
does not exist. These lines in black
drawn from the weirs downstream
offer the general shape of the country
but must not be regarded as accurate.

# HOW A MARK VII TRENCH MORTAR FUSE IS LIKE LOVE

There are two kinds of Mark VII Trench Mortar Fuse:
delay and non-delay. The head
of the delay fuse is painted black and the detonator
socket is painted violet. The head of the non-delay fuse
is painted white, while the detonator socket is left
unpainted.
        Just below the shoulder
of the upper section of the fuse body
are the threads by which the fuse is attached
to the adapter in the shell which is, in turn,
screwed into the detonator socket,
which is made of brass.
           In early morning light
on the tapered surface of each body
you will find a stamp with the name
of the fuse, the length of delay, the lot number,
the initials of the loader.

# THE ERROR OF THE DAY OR MOMENT

> "Without knowledge of the 'error of the day or moment' (caused by wind, temperature, humidity and barometric pressure), shooting 'from the map,' that is, at targets that could not be observed by the battery, was often a waste of time and ammunition."
> —Peter Chasseaud, *Artillery's Astrologers* (57–58).

The error of the day or moment
is not something I did
or didn't do.

Every day, every moment
has its error.

Today, for example,
the sly heat
when you're close.
The thickness
of the air that slows
shells and alters
birdsong.
The lacunae
in reports.

The error is not ours.

The error
is something
we must be given.

## SUMMARY OF INTELLIGENCE
Night of 3 October 1917
Trench map sheet 28 NE 1 Zonnebeke


Patrols reported the goddess
Paldan Lhamo in the vicinity of D.28.d.2.1
at 0245. She is sometimes called
*queen of the sickles* or *great life mistress*.
The body was dark blue, and lean, with one face,
four hands, two feet, wearing
ox-skin and a diadem
of bone ornament and ash. Spattered
with specks of fat she carried a sack
of diseases, a trident, and a pair of dice.
The patrol saw *she* and *hell* arise
from the turquoise seed-syllable
*shell* and working parties tonight, despite
anticipated rain, will dig, linking
her deep, round footprints
across featureless terrain.

## ADDITIONAL INFORMATION

When the men looked
at the horses' cheeks they saw
color come into the world
and because of that everything
including a horizon
became possible.

This was not reported.

# THE MISSING

As unexploded
shells are, sometimes
coughed up
by earth, greeted
gingerly. Mostly
cap badge and jaw.

## BUT YOU KNEW THIS

An obstacle or entanglement must be broad enough
to not be easily bridged and must be near enough
to be effectively watched at night.

To maintain the obstacle or entanglement
constant care is required. It must be inspected
every night. Resources should be assigned,

permanently, to its repair and improvement.
Every effort must be taken to conceal and protect it;
this is best done by sinking it in hollows or trenches.

Because close and constant observation will be required
loopholes are deemed to be essential.
Build them into your first line.

## WHAT SHE TOLD ME
Wieltje Farm Cemetery
26 October 2014
Trench map sheet 28 NW 2 St. Julien C.28.a.5.5


*Girl, keep to these haunted places.*
*Carry what you dare not.*

*Cut your fetters. Give up attachments.*
*Find what here says inside you.*

*You are not here to verify,*
*Instruct yourself, inform curiosity*

*Or carry report. You are here to kneel*
*Where fear has been valid.*

"Gentlemen, we may not make history tomorrow, but we shall certainly change the geography."

—Major-General Charles Harington, Chief of Staff to General Herbert Plumer (2nd Army, Commanding), on the evening of 6 June 1917, hours before nineteen mines were detonated under the Messines Ridge.


"The continuing alteration of the ground makes it difficult to reconcile a vision of terrain at one point in time with its appearance at another. . . . This is not to say that under these circumstances one does not keep trying to see."

—Mark D. Larabee, *Front Lines of Modernism: Remapping the Great War in British Fiction.* (New York, Palgrave MacMillan, St. Martin's Press, 2011. 27.)

## NOTES ON THE INTERPRETATION OF AEROPLANE PHOTOGRAPHS

Examine the ground in the photograph
as an item of independent evidence.
                              Compare this evidence
with reports of visual observation, locations given in Intelligence
                                        Summaries,
and evidence from reliable prisoners.

Eliminate those portions of this evidence which are obviously song.

                              Consider the likely places
for the objects referred to in credible reports,
and verify them.

Do not allow yourself to read in the photograph what you *want* to see.

            Compare the photograph
with earlier photographs of the same locality.
It is from such comparisons that valuable results are obtained.

This applies in particular to the appearance of objects as affected by
                                        the passage of time.

## CONSTRUCTION OF TRENCH SYSTEMS:
## EXPLANATION OF DIAGRAM #7

In the first line two companies:
one company in support line,
one company in reserve.
Double line of trenches
in the first or firing line;
double line
of trenches in support;
communication and cover trenches
behind the firing trenches
of the first line,
support lines,
and in strong points.
Also, in places, dummy trenches.
Two distinct lines
of wire entanglement
in front of the first line.
The whole supporting point divided
into two longitudinal
sections, each protected in flank
by wire,
and each protected
with firing trenches
faced to the rear
as well as to front
and flanks.
Passages through the wire
of the first line
made continuous through the two lines,
but always in the reentrants.
Listening posts
in front of each firing trench
of the first line,
placed between the two systems
of wire.

Machine guns of the first line
in reentrants,
those on the flanks
to sweep the intervals
between this center of resistance
and those adjacent.
Communication and approach trenches
provided with firing parapets
mostly facing outward toward the wire
of each section
of the supporting point. Now try
to find your
way back through
all this in
the dark.

## AMULET AGAINST MADNESS

This amulet protects the wearer against madness.

The image is drawn on paper, backed with linen, on the 15th of a suitable month. It consists of a smiling bull-headed creature with its eyes turned to the right, seven snakes as hair, and two human heads above its own. The first human head is terror-stricken, the second peaceful with a ribbon flowing from its crown. Both of the creature's hands are raised to the level of the chest and hold a *phurba* with a flaming blade, which pierces a triangular form at the level of the navel. Above the triangular form is the seed syllable *ACK*. The lower part of the body is coiled like concertina wire.

It is smeared with different medicines and worn on the body.

## AMULET AGAINST GROUND DEITIES

This amulet protects the wearer against evils resulting from turning the soil, digging holes, moving stones or cutting trees, and similar activities which may offend *sa bdag*, *gzhi bdag*, and other local ground deities.

The image is drawn on paper or linen with ink made from crushed lead mixed with water. It is of a chained turtle, on a bed of clouds, whose 5.9 mm shell bears a clockwise spiral incantation consisting of syllables and the name of your specific location.

The image is wrapped together with a piece of iron-blade with nine little holes and placed in a canister. The canister is a tinned iron box reinforced with ribs. Inside it, grains of chemical compounds are packed loosely to permit the passage of air through the canister and are supported by a curved wire screen. The elbow tube connects the canister with the mouthpiece, which is made of pure gum rubber. The eyepieces are made of celluloid or of specially prepared glass, and can be cleaned by means of folds in the material.

All of this must be placed in a satchel worn with the snap fasteners facing toward the body. It must be carried outside of all other equipment. When over two miles from the front line it may be worn slung over the right shoulder.

## CHILLED FEET

Chilled feet and frostbite
are caused by prolonged standing
in cold water and mud
were our constant companions.
These conditions can be prevented or diminished
by means of improved trench construction; by reducing
the time spent in trenches; by movement;
by the provision of warmth, shelter, hot food,
and facilities for washing the feet and drying wet clothes
were nowhere to be found.
Boots, socks, and puttees are to be removed
at least once in 24 hours, the feet rubbed
for 20 minutes, dried, greased with whale oil,
and a dry pair of socks put on, if available.
On no account must the feet be held near a fire
would have been a godsend
nor must hot water be used.

## ACTUAL THINGS WITH CHARACTERISTICS
Northwest of Quebec Farm
20 September 1917
Trench map sheet 20 SE 3 Poelcappelle V.25.d.2.1


If individuals have no psychic or magical abilities
then actual things with characteristics,
such as the four elements, hail, poison, boils, precipices,
and so on, become obstacles.

Whenever such forms arise,
remain in a state
of detachment and integrate them
into your path as illusions.

Yesterday, when actual things with characteristics arose,
a detachment tried to integrate them into its path
as illusions, but the actual things with characteristics
were stubborn and well-led.

# THE OBSTACLE

The lush green didn't move. An obstacle
that wasn't there lay ahead of me.
There had been rain.
                It was the memory of an obstacle,
unmarked on my modern map, waiting,
its shining barbed coils dripping in the morning air.

An advance had been anticipated here.

All around it the beginning of the day swirled, as if
my sudden attention to it, struggling with its dimensions,
was another wave of confusion
in khaki, and then what always followed:
the waverings, occluded, falling to pieces, their lines
now only to indicate elevation. . . .

If I change my position
it becomes easier to see. Shadowed by the edge of the wood,
lying low, coiling and recoiling itself, practicing.
Each time waking itself with its sharp reminders.
Every now and then the sound of a car passing. Around it
full summer crowding into what should be
a black-and-white photograph—*protection*—
the vacationing family again, on bicycles, moving
unhindered and quickly.

It refuses to look,
patient, waiting, resisting, resisting
still the very idea of advance. Patient,
but without compassion. And I
still near the edge of the field, of the wood,
between the field and the wood, waiting
for some gap, a way through.

Then some kind of flare hovering
illuminating the daylight, filling the hollowed ground, then
implacable endurance, the residual
stubbornly held on to, history
again material, catching
at my clothes—some kind of affirmation—
until there it is, all of it—spider wire, snarls
of concertina, knife rests, chevaux-de-frise,
until the thing itself—as seen here
or from the air, quivering, spooling
back on itself, revealing the rest, where it was—
is for a moment clear.

## HARM
Just north of Railway Wood
Trench map sheet 28 NW 4 Ypres


We are no longer confused about harm.

Harm is in specific locations.
I.5.d.9.1, for example, the small field
100 yards due east of Gully Farm.

We strive to remain unattached,
without attraction or aversion
to material forms.
                    The way
Phillips and Mercer did,
who understood such distinctions.

Most of them is still missing.

## PRELIMINARY ORDERS
Second Army, X Corps, 21st Division, 62nd Infantry Brigade, 1 October 1917


The two lead companies will advance as light
as possible and thus will not carry shovels.

Nothing superfluous will be taken. No greatcoats
at Zero. Wire is reported to be light.

Bayonets will not be fixed
if there is moonlight.

Protecting walls must be built for the horses at once.
The men may dig down or build walls for themselves.


If the two lead companies advance as light
they will not need to advance as something else,

as men or fodder or exhortation or as a dark wing
that strains to unpin itself from wet ground.

If in moonlight bayonets will not be fixed
they can remain fluid, imagining themselves

as silver fear or unborn phosphor or even the wire out there
that is also reported to be light.


At Zero the warm enormous horses
will shrug their great coats behind protecting walls.

Try to imagine that the men will not need
to dig or build, but simply,

as the flares and star shells do,
advance as light.

## AMULET AGAINST DISCOVERY

This amulet protects the wearer from discovery.

It is a dull disk of careless alloy, at its center the seed syllable *TOC* encircled by a necklace of orders and guarded in the cardinal directions by a newborn mule, coordinates, an entrail, and a triangle of error.

It is folded and placed inside a prism that refracts sound.

"This [document] repeals, in so far as it concerns battle maps, properly so called, 'The Instructions on the Organization of Heavy Artillery Fire and the Preparation of Battle Maps for Fire,' of November 10, 1914. Those instructions had laid down the first principles for the preparation of battle maps, but they had considered their use principally for artillery fire."

—*Instructions Concerning Battle Maps*. (Washington, D.C.: Army War College, May 1917. 5.)

"They have a curious way of finding direction in Belgium. The landscape has no salient features of its own; everything blasted to mud—railway embankments, woods, roads confused in shell-holes and mine craters. Trees are only skeletons, and masses of obscene ruins mark farms or houses. You look in vain for a wood where such is marked on the map. The only way at night is to bend down close to the ground and gaze at the skyline for black shadows of pill-boxes; by those shadows you find your way. Or, to remember a road once shown, the oddest details must be noted—a solitary length of rail or wire, a 'dud' shell, three stakes together, a fragmentary hedge, a deserted water-logged trench, dead men lying at various angles, and the position of pill-boxes in relation to the track followed."

—Hugh Quigley, *Passchendaele and the Somme: A Diary of 1917*. (London: Associated Book Publishers Ltd., 1928. 125–126.)

## INDIRECT FIRE: SHOOTING FROM THE MAP
## (FROM APPENDIX B)

7.0   If you do not know where you are, use a plane table to locate your position by resection.

  7.1   Originally a plain table. Reflecting its simplicity.

    7.1.1   Cover the table with zinc (impervious to heat or cold) and on it mount a sheet of drawing paper. Carefully draw the map grid by hand on the mounted paper and then cut up the map itself into squares and gum them down, fitting each piece into its correct position on the corresponding grid underneath.

    7.1.2   The distortion of the paper due to gumming causes slight irregularities and overlaps in the piecing together but across the entire map there will be no accumulation of error.

  7.2   Resection. Here, not in the sense of cutting something away, of surgically removing a portion of an organ or tissue.*

8.0   Pick a point from which three previously fixed points can be seen.

  8.1   OK. Here, by the car. Then

  8.2   the memorial to the 85th Battalion (Nova Scotia Highlanders) at D.12.c.1.3,

  8.3   the prayer flag above the stupa outside the cave on the northeast spur of Copper Mountain, and

  8.4   where you were last seen that morning.

9.0   Orient the table by compass (the one with its error), and from the three fixed points draw back rays. Not lines (ours, theirs, these). Not arrows. Rays. Not to be basked in.

---

* Cf. "In the Soft Parts of the Body," p. 61.

9.1 If these three rays pass through a point, this point is your position.

    9.1.1 Were this the case then, with this map, fire might be brought to bear onto the object of desire that cannot be observed directly.

    9.1.2 You can hear the Wind Horse moving among the willows.

9.2 If they do not pass through a point, the rays will form a small triangle called the "triangle of error."

    9.2.1 Again, although small and here contained, error. And, I think, fear.

9.3 Your true position can be determined by the following rules:

    9.3.1 If the "triangle of error" is inside the triangle formed by the three fixed points, your position is inside the triangle of error; and if it is outside, your position is outside the triangle of error.

        9.3.1.1 For many years I thought this section

            9.3.1.1.1 these "triangles" and triangles and positions inside and outside fixed or not with their "error" or error taken singly or together or perhaps in sequence

            9.3.1.1.2 describing what is inside as inside or outside as outside, creating for me confusions about what I now know are actually separate (as in two different) triangles, one made by points one by the rays themselves

        9.3.1. made no sense, but was either a printing error or charm.

    9.3.2 In the latter case the position will be such that it is either to the left of all the rays when facing the fixed points, or to the right of them all.

    9.3.3 Of the six realms formed by the rays, there are only two in which this condition can be fulfilled.

9.3.3.1 These are the realms of humans and of the hungry ghosts (*preta*).

9.3.3.2 The latter are immaterial beings, unsatisfied and restless, desperate and famished, wandering endlessly across the ground between unfixed positions, nursing their error.

9.3.4 Your exact position is determined by the condition that its distances from the rays must be proportional to the length of the rays, i.e. the position on the sketch must be nearest to that side of the triangle formed by the shortest ray, and farthest from that formed by the longest ray.

9.3.4.1 [This section intentionally left blank.]

9.4 Having thus determined your position, place the sight rule along the line joining it and the most distant of the points used; set the sight rule on the point by revolving the plane table; clamp and test the other two points. If there is still an error (which should, however, be much smaller), go through the process again.

# INVERTED MAPS

As a rule it was North
up and scale
consistent from
sheet to sheet

but for a few weeks
early on certain
sheets had
German batteries

up—disorienting
for us but exactly how
it looked
to the guns.

## SHE EXPLAINS HOW TO RECOGNIZE THE SIGNS OF SPECIFIC SPIRITS AND DEMONS WHEN THEY ARISE
Menin Road, 23 September 1917

*You are in the midst of much filth, or going along a road,*
*or digging up earth, or escorting, or loading*
*or unloading goods. Many people try to harm you*
*or you are trying to help them. The sky fills with fire,*
*or lights of many different colors fall from the sky*
*like a rain of arrows.*
                    *Your tongue is so dry you can't speak,*
*or you feel uneasy. You become senseless in a thick darkness, your limbs are stuck*
*outstretched or flexed, or your skin hardens and contracts, your body becomes*
*numb and prickly, or it boils and burns like a bonfire, or it feels intense nausea*
*like ants running out.*
                    *There are human corpses*
*burned or stacked up. Many pack animals are loaded up and led around.*
*New and old things cover the whole place. There are many horse corpses*
*burned or spread around or flayed and chopped up. Small animals*
*are eating them. The whole ground consists of human and horse skin, or it is filled*
*with many fresh and stale heads.*

*These are the outer signs.*

## STAND TO

Now that you have gone you are forbidden
to tell me where you are.

I live on Field Service Post Cards,
reverie, and the belief
that we are inviolable and eternal
and matter. The big
invulnerable words.

What I want are the soft parts of your body.

Where I stood watch, at your flank, alert,
behind the warm berm of your rib,
close as breath, looking
out at the blank expanse
you would have to cross.

When I think of you my whole body
says *fire.*

## NEAR WURST FARM
2 October 1917


At some point you could see through the broken ground and it became an interior filled with the limitless, a terrible smell, and surprise.

Instructions scatter and were of little use but the unsystematic often brought back a quiver of intelligence at first light while through the periscope nothing, imminent but slowly.

Near where we used to sit playing cards with tedium and panic most of the men are smoking. I cannot remember what she told me to do when I see this.

## AMULET AGAINST CAMOUFLAGE

This amulet enables the wearer to detect and see through camouflage.

It consists of fragments of apprehension and crushed glass, moistened with rain. No syllables are used.

When placed inside a small section of freshwater reed and worn on the body, a copse becomes transparent, netting and paint peel away from the long guns, loopholes gape among sandbags, and what tracks say becomes visible from the air.

## SIGNATURES

Not simply gun emplacement, ammunition dump, or redoubt,
but any such work in relation to other work,
and the beaten paths between them:
a railway line that breaks into a different gauge,
a cone of blast mark on snow, an abnormal
bend in the trench line, saps, corduroy roads,
fortified shell-holes, an absence of shadows,
a shape or alignment unlikely
to be found in nature.
                    The presence, absence, appearance,
and configuration of such works form a signature
from which could be read not only position and disposition
but intent:
              what was about to happen
giving me its name, one that could be read from the air,
but not now or from here.

## BEFORE THE ATTACK ON POELCAPPELLE
5 October 1917

The daily telegram from the Meteorological Section contained the error of the day or moment, that detailed barometric pressure, temperature, wind speed and direction on the ground and at various altitudes. It also contained a forecast.

This latter is what I want to have been changed.

A spot should have been found where water spirits (*klu*) dwell: by a small stream or, if there had been a large pond or shell crater nearby, on its western edge. A broken helmet or mule skull filled with maps and sketches of the area to be protected should have been buried on raised ground that lay in the direction from which rain was most likely to approach. On top of it they should have built a stone cairn crowned with thread crosses made with brown and black wool.

She has a smoke-colored body. She holds a raven, an axe, a field dressing, and a leather pouch filled with wind. On her right shoulder sits a falcon of iron with turquoise eyes. She tries to comfort me. She says,

> *You want the water*
> *to have prevented itself.*
> *To have aligned with them against*
> *its own increase. To have seen*
> *itself as an error.*

## OBSTACLES

Ignorance (*avidya*). Attachment. Aversion. Wire.
Felled trees. Inundations. Clinging to life (*abhinivesha*).

Whether an obstacle can be seen from the air
depends on the length of time it has been in place.

At certain times of day
grief can be seen.

The surface of the ground beneath an obstacle
that has been protected from traffic and weather
will show as a dark shadow

accentuated by light lines across it
wherever there has been or is a track through.

PERISCOPE

At sunrise, across fields of broken chalk, pairs of mirrors come to light.
Again it is possible to see through the earth and around corners.


This is one way the lines reflect each other,
also the mist beginning to stir, unfamiliar every single time.


The tiny area shown on the map flattens in the men's hands and its
certainties begin to rub off.
A lark is not concerned, and this helps.


It is very cold, and memory, with bits of what happened floating just
beneath the surface,
has almost reached the top of their boots.

## AMULET AGAINST DISMEMBERMENT

This amulet protects the wearer against dismemberment.

It consists of two rolled lengths of linen, each attached to a pad of absorbent material. The inner surface of the pad is folded so that the surface is protected from contact with the fingers. A safety pin is lightly stitched to each roll and is folded in waxed paper to protect it. These pads and rolls are enclosed in a waterproof outer covering which is sealed hermetically by means of a gummed edge.

A small ampoule of iodine is enclosed in a cardboard tube, and is placed between the two sealed packages, the whole being enclosed in a khaki cloth covering, on which instructions for use are printed.

It is sewn into a small pocket on the inner side of the tunic at the left corner of the skirt of the coat.

## SOUND RANGING

The colonel
was confusing
the shock wave
caused by the shell
passing at more
than the speed of
sound with the sound
of the gun
itself.
     The way
in certain circumstances
abdominal recoil
is mistaken
for grief: shock
preceding report.

## THE BATTLE OF POELCAPPELLE

Nothing of Nicholson's shivering.
Nor the way in which Haxton slipped back through the gaps in the wire.
                              (Could these be seen from the air?)

Then a string of inexplicable postponements and the rain tapering off.

Meanwhile a piece of what happened on the left, among the East
                                                    Lancashires,
                              (Had they broken?)
builds itself into the story,
                    the way this afternoon in early October offers,
                                        many years later,
a theory of what happened and then waits, curious
to test it against what I want to see
                              (Are they here or not?),
and will decide whether that moment can be fixed.


                    While some mechanism to mark time—
passing cars, or the advance of the barrage—
suggests an irrevocable moving forward
in a line unbroken
                    (as ordered, as imagined),
and underneath it reveals other postponements bearing, gently,
other possibilities, other gaps in the story,
and perhaps, this time, Miller, on the stretcher between them.

## NIGHT: SHELL-HOLE
Southwestern edge of Decoy Wood
12 October 1917
Trench map sheet 28 NE 1 Zonnebeke D.18.a.2.1


Because I am terrified I reach out in the darkness and touch another man's body.

He is solid, and protection, and unaware of me lying beneath him.

His remains are very still, and this helps.

It is cold and the water seems to rise very slowly.

He is both a man and a caution, here for a reason.

I will wait for daylight to see where we are.

The way his arm is folded, rigid with cold, offers a loophole, a way to see, undetected, and this may open out onto some kind of actionable intelligence that might be kept, carried back, and, in some small way, matter.

I have been warned several times about this, the risks, what might happen if I raise my head.

## NIGHT: BEDROOM
London
14 October 1917


Because you are missing I reach out in the darkness and touch another man's body.

He is solid, and protection, and unaware of me weeping beneath him.

He remains very still, and this helps.

It is cold.

He is both a man and a desperation, here for a reason.

Perhaps in daylight someone will see where you are.

His folded limbs act as a blind, a way not to see, and this evasion opens out onto some kind of imagined evidence that things might remain as they were and, in some small way, matter.

I was warned several times about this, the risks, what might happen if you raised your head.

# NOTES ON THE INTERPRETATION OF AEROPLANE
PHOTOGRAPHS


Concentrate your whole mind
on the particular object(s) you are seeking.

Do not let your attention wander to subsidiary objectives.
Follow every traverse and detail with your pointer
in regular and logical order.

The signs of wind dissolving into space
are a darkening of some areas
and black splotches on the external body.

The inner signs are a bright radiance
like the light in a cloudless sky.

Ascertain the direction of light:

shadow plays a most important part
in trying to decide whether the circular shape you see
is convex or concave.

At just such a point all the great fears come.

## THE GUTS OF IT

I think I would prefer
to be killed in a railway
accident he said Why Because
well there you are

                    but
if you're killed by an exploding
shell he went on then
where the hell
are you

# IN THE SOFT PARTS OF THE BODY

wounds from large fragments or entire projectiles
show extensive and deep contusions, crushing, a tearing
away of tissue. They are vast
erosions, deep furrows, large lesions often with significant
pieces of flesh hanging, fimbriated,
ecchymotic, contused, and frequently, in their deep parts, complicated
by metallic foreign bodies, by earth, by fragments
of clothing and thus doomed to suppuration and grave
complications, gangrene and
tetanus, for example.
                    For such wounds use a simple *mda' dar*
fletched with crow, with a slender point of polished copper,
and its shaft painted red. To its feathered end
attach five narrow lengths of silk—yellow, white, red, blue, and green—
and three sheep-bone dice. Move a mirror
along the patient's body until it reaches the source of his pain.
At this exact location set the arrow with its point
touching the wound and begin
to suck at the other end of the shaft.
                    In this way, clots of blood,
free splinters of shrapnel, and all tissue that has lost its vitality
are removed. Wipe the wound surface with a pad soaked
in permanganate of potassium and then apply an ointment
containing corrosive sublimate, salol, antipyrine, carbolic acid,
and iodoform, with Vaseline as an excipient.

## RECOGNIZING THE SIGNS OF DEATH
44th Casualty Clearing Station, Poperinghe


dreaming of being led by a man on foot
or on a horse, toward the west

in the shade of trees, where one cannot
be escorted by others, and once there

hearing someone crying behind one

then the rustle of stiff cloth, light breaking,
the muffled sound of metal on metal

a woman nearby carries burning twigs of juniper
and a mirror

## FIELD SERVICE POSTCARD

NOTHING IS TO BE WRITTEN
*unless I have crossed this out*
I am
quite well
have been admitted into hospital
am sick wounded going on well hope
*I send you*
EXCEPT THE DATE AND SIGNATURE
*I don't see another option*
to be discharged soon I
SENTENCES NOT REQUIRED MAY BE
am being
ERASED
sent down to
have received your letter telegram parcel
have received no
lately for a long time
SIGNATURE ONLY

## THE RELIEF

After days facing
pestilence bags, blue
and red yarn-ball
weapons, bat skins, and the long
black-beaked cemetery birds
we were relieved on the 1st
at 5 p.m. by the remains
of 7th Division's South Staffords.

"At the place called BROODSEINDE take the Ypres-Roulers road on the left, to visit the ruins of ZONNEBEKE.

Zonnebeke was taken in 1914 by the Germans, who made an outpost of it in front of their lines. The village was recaptured on September 26 [1917], then lost in April, 1918, and finally retaken in the following October.

Return to the fork (which was commanded by numerous small forts) and turn to the left: military cemetery by the side of the road. In the fields on the right, 200 yards beyond the level crossing, there is a monument to the memory of 148 officers and men of the Canadian 85th Battalion.

Passing through shell-torn country, PASSCHENDAELE—now razed to the ground—is reached. All that remains of the church is the mound seen in the background of the photograph.

Passchendaele was captured by the Germans in November, 1914, and later by the British (October 26, 1917). The village had already been wiped out by the bombardment, but the position, which dominated Ypres and Roulers, was an important one. The fighting there was of the fiercest, Hindenburg having ordered it to be held at all costs."

—*Ypres and the Battles for Ypres: 1914–1918. An Illustrated History and Guide.* (Michelin Illustrated Guides to the Battlefields (1914–1918). Clermont-Ferrand: Michelin & Cie., 1919. 63–64.)

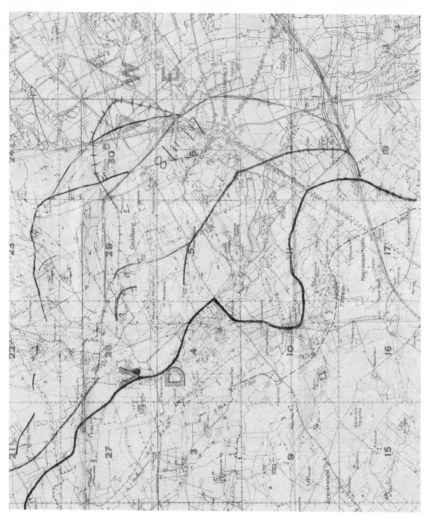

*Final Passchendaele Offensive (detail)*
*British and Canadian lines annotated to 8 November 1917*

## AMULET AGAINST DISAPPEARANCE

This amulet protects the wearer against disappearing.

I place it in your hair.

## WAR DIARY, 7TH INFANTRY BRIGADE,
## 3RD CANADIAN DIVISION
28 October 1917

Fair with ground mists. At 3:00 p.m. the battalion moved off from
YPRES to the RED HOUSE OF COPPER MOUNTAIN via YARL-
HATSE and on the way subjugated 128 haunted places. Battalion ar-
rived at GRAVENSTAFEL AREA relieving the 9th Brigade to attack
2nd objective in the PASSCHENDAELE offensive. No. 1 Co'y relieving
the 43rd, No. 2 Co'y the 52nd, and No. 3 Co'y the 58th Battalion, No.
4 Co'y being temporarily attached to the 49th Battalion but taking up
their position on the front from which we were to attack and relieving
the 116th Battalion in DAD TRENCH. The local spirit ZANGRI KYIL
came and avowed his resolve for awakening and promised to protect
the doctrine. The Meteo Office is predicting difficulty breathing and
a rain of weapons.

# INSTRUCTIONS FOR WORKING WITH THE *GYALPO*
Southeast of the Gravenstafel-Mosselmarkt Road
Trench map sheet 28 NE 1 Zonnebeke D.10.b.5.7


*Water overflow, or calm turbid water,*
*covers everything in a whole area.*
*You are sinking, or naturally alarmed and afraid,*
*or you become terrified thinking that you have to get across the ground.*
*You feel love and compassion for the many trees*
*and mules and men that lie under the water.*
*You are blown about in swirling rains of dirt and stone*
*and these obstruct your view.*
*Fire intensifies in the air and almost burns you.*
*A white light in the sky the size of a shield*
*drifts all around. You are enveloped in brown storm winds*
*or caught inside the light, and so on.*

*These are the secret signs or indications of the* gyalpo.
*Any person should be able to readily identify*
*whatever indications occur as I have explained*
*without mixing them up.*
*If you don't recognize them, then there is no way*
*to work with the* gyalpo. *By being undistracted*
*and unmistaken you can implement*
*the meditative absorption of their harassment.*
*Do not ignore even little outer apparitions.*

*This is the esoteric instruction on working with the* gyalpo.

# FURTHER INSTRUCTIONS

5 November 1917, 11:45 p.m.
Trench map sheet 28 NE 1 Zonnebeke


After the power-suppression ceremony
has been completed by the artillery
and you have reached the center of the village
at D.6.d.4.5 and have consolidated
in that terrifying place
summon as your guests all
who seek to harm you, all
who damage thoughts, all
who set obstacles before you,
all that you don't know, all that you see
incorrectly, all that haunts
that specific location. All of these,
and all sentient beings of the three realms,
have been your parents.
Cherish them.

# TELEPHONE REPORTS:
## 2ND CANADIAN DIVISIONAL ARTILLERY
Zero Hour, 6:00 a.m., 6 November 1917

6:01 a.m.  Barrage opened sharp and on time and appeared to be very uniform.

6:03 a.m.  Sky filled with rainbow light, flowers of various colors rained down. Sound of cymbals reverberated against the sky.

6:06 a.m.  Shelling on our batteries, light, in D.14.

6:10 a.m.  Orange rockets on Corp on left. Dump in ZONNEBEKE set on fire.

6:19 a.m.  Bosche put up last flares and lights on our Front. Many golden and chain greens on our Flanks.

6:20 a.m.  Several white flares in the vicinity of the church, very clear and vivid. A soft rain wafted down and everything that was not already moist became slick.

6:49 a.m.  15 men seen working round the crest of Hill 55 at V.30.a NE of PASSCHENDAELE village.

6:54 a.m.  One of our planes active on our Front dropping lights. Soft fingers of mist shimmered, light naturally formed into mirage-like shapes.

6:58 a.m.  Party of men coming out on left apparently prisoners.

7:02 a.m.  In sky, about a spear's length away, matted cloud of various colors, the nature of light.

7:08 a.m.  1st Division seen going over ridge.

8:05 a.m.  28th Battalion, hidden in the basic space of the sky, reported they have gained all objectives and are consolidating. Casualties heavy.

"The events on which our orders would depend were taking place about a mile as the crow flies, to our right front, on top of the slope that rose before us. We could not see anything of them, and no news or rumor came our way; but without a knowledge of these events an account of our later concerns would be meaningless."

—Capt. J. C. Dunn, D.S.O., M.C. and Bar, D.C.M., 2nd Battalion, His Majesty's 23rd Foot, The Royal Welsh Fusiliers, *The War the Infantry Knew, 1914–1919*. (London: 1938. 231.)

"The wounded came back to give vague hints of what was happening, but as a rule wounded men know nothing more than their own adventures in their own track or shell-craters. Some of them have never come back. No man knows yet what has become of them out there. Little groups may still be holding on to advanced posts out there in the swamps."

—Dispatch of 31 October 1917. Philip Gibbs, *From Bapaume to Passchendaele, 1917*. (London: William Heinemann, 1918. 373.)

# THE MISSING: THE OUTER SIGNS

Rifles or stakes protruding
from the ground
bearing helmets or equipment;

partial remains or equipment
on the surface or protruding
from the ground;

on the surface
rat holes near
pieces of bone or equipment;

discoloration: grass
will be vivid blue-
green with broader

blades, earth and
water a greenish
or gray color.

## THE MISSING: THE INNER SIGNS

Gasp, or spines protruding
from the heart
bearing grief or sunset;

the partial imprint of your
wrist or sunset protruding
from my heart;

in my throat
splinters
of joy or amulet;

distortion: knives
are a vivid blue-
green with broader

blades, earth and
water an empty
or gray color.

# THE MISSING: THE SECRET SIGNS

Greatcoat, prayer beads, or bone
drum hanging
from a poplar;

from the feet
up the coarse body
vanishing

into this multicolored
light leaving
no corpse behind;

dissolution: nails
and hair and these
here only

owing to
my thirst
for relics.

## RECOGNIZING THE SIGNS THAT AN AMULET HAS FAILED

Splintered corduroy roads.

A village, less than a heap of bricks, erased altogether by three inches
of snow.

A mask, repairing itself.

Hail.

The same surroundings at dusk, closing in also.

The Summary riddled with conflicting errors.

Careful weeping on the other side of the traverse.

A man in a felt hat with markings walking slowly in a northerly direc-
tion carrying a tin pail.

A silence between when I ask and dusk.

Then the flutter of tiny papers
flushed from a small wood.

## MAP AND GROUND

At some point
map and ground
part company.
The lines
cannot be found
either.
Then as now
even where you were
is lost.

## FIELD SURVEY

Part of then
fell into a different sector

one boundary
the canal

a moment waiting
for the aerial photos

This traffic circle
was Hellfire corner

If this is true
what else must be true

## THE MISSING

Some became smoke, cloud, and rain:

      as when a pot breaks
      the space within and the space without
      become intermingled
               the body reduced
      to its atomic constituents indistinguishable
      from the awareness within

Others dissolved into light from their feet upwards:

      the heavy shelling at D.6.d.4.5
      west of what remained of the church
      for example
               and after the light
      faded from the sky there were no bodies

So it is said
         that instead of wooden crosses they have names
planted in space

# MACHIK LAPDRÖN TRIES TO EXPLAIN ONE
# OF THE IMMEASURABLES
Inauguration of the Menin Gate Memorial to the Missing
24 July 1927


*These mothers who have been so kind to us, who are so bound up with cherishing,*
*are unhappy and pained with suffering.*

*They should carefully investigate whether or not the bodies and minds and sufferings*
*of those beings who are the object of attachment had any real existence.*

*They don't understand that all phenomena lack even a hair's tip of true existence,*
*that they are like a dream or an illusion.*

*These mothers have not gained self-control over their own consciousness,*
*so violent afflictive emotions control them, and they live like crazy people.*

*In this wretched state, they don't have a single ray of hope or place of refuge.*

*There isn't even a moment of respite from the suffering that they experience like*
*the torrent of a river.*

*If you know all objects of attachment to be like a dream or illusion,*
*if you are free of fixation to material existence,*
*that is called immeasurable joy.*

> The woman hears none of this.
>
> She looks up at the last
> name and first initial
> of her nonexistent son.

*Considering this,*
*meditate to the point of tears.*

# GIVEN A NORMALLY FINE AUGUST

from *Dispatch #4 to the War Cabinet, London*
Sir Douglas Haig, Commanding-in-Chief, British Armies in the Field
25 December 1917


The year was far spent.
The weather
consistently unpropitious.
And the state of the ground
in consequence of rain
and shelling combined
made movement
inconceivably difficult.

Though the condition of the ground
continued to deteriorate, the weather
then became unsettled
rather than persistently wet
and thus progress had not yet
become impossible.

Given a normally fine August
the capture of the whole ridge
within the space
of a few weeks was well
within the power
of the men
who achieved so much.

"Camouflage is the art of concealing that something is concealed. Its keynote is deception. By it, objects are rendered indistinguishable or unrecognizable by means of a covering or disguise. Concealment, in the limited sense of hiding from view, is screening not camouflage."

—The War Office, *Manual of Field Works (All Arms). 1921. (Provisional.)* (London: His Majesty's Stationery Office, 1921. 93.)

# CAMOUFLAGE: TRENCHES

The way a new trench
is best concealed by making it look like
an abandoned one and an abandoned one
is best concealed by making it look like
a meadow, or a digression, say,
one that has cast off its lines
and is moving slowly away from us
downriver, and is just now—see?—passing
under a bridge, making its way to the coast,
and as it drifts through the small trading towns
no one who sees it thinks to ask why
it was held or who had been there.

## BELOW BELLEVUE SPUR

The ground is so alive, now,
with its waves of corn, its glossy cows,

the scattered happiness of wrens
busy among poplars.

Walk with me, barefoot,
along the narrow edge of this vast sea

of in-this-moment green.
Look for shells.

# THE SECOND LAW OF OCCLUSION

Looking down a convex slope from a given point
one's line of sight cannot fall at a steeper gradient
than that of the ground.

        (One cannot see *through* the ground).

            Thus the lower part of the slope
will be unseen, or "dead." For this reason a convex slope
is ill-suited for defense: the enemy
will be out of sight and not exposed to fire
while crossing dead ground.
            Even if your map
is firmly anchored to the trig skeleton
and is corrected to the present moment
and shows a slope below a crest to be concave
you must inspect it. The ground.
Personally.

        (This is what I have been trying to do.)

        It is possible that this ground
is alive, the men also. But I can't see them. Some extravagant
convexity. Or light bent
by the gravity of a body or by some quantum law
that says I can see a man or his movement
but not both.

# INDIRECT FIRE: SHOOTING FROM THE MAP
## (FROM APPENDIX B)

10.0 In summary, your best position is inside the triangle formed by the three fixed points (assuming they are points, fixed, and can be seen) of which two are near and one is distant. (Note this is not to be confused with the triangle of error.) Accuracy of position is insured by aligning on the distant point. Generally: Fix from near points. (Me. Here. Then.) Set by a distant point. (You. There. Them.)

    10.1 When there are a number of points, any three of which may be used for resection purposes (there are so many points, and so much that cannot be observed directly), recollect in choosing the point to be used that:

        10.1.1 When the three points chosen, and your position, lie on or near the circumference of a circle, the accurate determination of your position is not possible by this method.

        10.1.2 The three points chosen should be such that the rays from them do not intersect at acute angles and thereby make a badly shaped triangle of error.

    10.2 It will have been noticed that the compass is only used to orient the plane table approximately, and that the final fixing does not at all depend on the compass.

    10.2.1 After all that.

11.0 At the going down of the sun, and in the morning, remember them.

# THAT ONE TIME, IN DECEMBER 1914

the goddess came to the place of hell
and just by seeing her the hell-laborers
delayed their torture work, and sentient beings
on both sides, all of us, were instantly freed
from anger and the results of anger
such as the sufferings of rain and cold,
hailstorms and broken sandbags, and being
pulled apart and chopped up.
The burning ground became
lapis lazuli and the hungry ghosts
were sated, the animals no longer suffered,
the demigods were no longer jealous
of one another and the gods
shredded all the maps.
All needs and desires fell away like rain
and the suffering of all sentient beings
stopped, went silent, and across the frozen ground
between us you could hear the carols.

## OUR BODIES

Our bodies grew younger, pliant, light,
like the ten winds or cotton wool,

changeless and radiantly luminous.
"We will be separated for just a moment."

When I looked over my shoulder
a dense mist where there had been coral and turquoise.

Your words were lies to me but not to you,
a promise incompletely informed,

as we are when we make a vow, in earnest or the moment,
all alloy of desire and blindness, suspended,

all wish embedded in the apotropaic,
the way the figure waits in clay, cooling slowly,

assuming he will be released back to daylight,
intact, by clearing parties or skilled craftsmen.

My body may have felt like a lie to you but not to me,
although there were lights in the dark air,

falling slowly, illuminating the ground below
where everything had stopped moving.

When I looked over my shoulder
the dense mist separated for just a moment

and there were our bodies,
changeless and radiantly luminous.

Your words begin to sound younger, pliant, light,
like the ten winds moving into the present.

When I look over your shoulder I see
the ground as an alloy of fire and blindness,

that we are separated for just a moment, and a dense mist
in which we are again coral and turquoise.

## WHAT SHE TOLD ME
Canadian Memorial at Crest Farm
Trench map sheet 28 NE 1 Zonnebeke D.12.a.2.9


*You have come back here without knowing why, or when, or from where.*
*You have come back here carefully, without instructions or faith.*
*You have come back here because there has been no other place*
*than this: where* now *does not exist, nor* then.

*See? Your footsteps on the ground are held by theirs.*
*See? You stood watch as they catch a few minutes of sleep.*

## 14 NOVEMBER 2017

Yesterday the regiment
came out of the line.
No matter what I did
it refused to stay. It shed its
supply train, ammunition column,
General Officer's motor car,
and other appurtenances of GHQ troops and
two days later went south
to 2nd Division's area at Béthune.

## AT GOUDBERG COPSE

Mother, send down blessings on this haunted place
where we tripped and fell over barbed

wire into trenches over stumps, rose
and tripped again the whole night through,

where we stumbled on terrible shapes, not flesh and blood forms
but made of a swarm of noxious black darkness.

We buried more than the strength
of the regiment on these terrible ridges.

Please hold us with unbiased compassion.
Hold with compassion the gods

and demons gathered here. Please stay here
and grant your blessings.

# AFTERWORD

When thinking of the literature of World War I, most poets and readers instinctively turn to the soldier poets of that time: Wilfred Owen, Robert Graves, Siegfried Sassoon, Isaac Rosenberg, Edmund Blunden, David Jones, among others, and may also glance at some noble noncombatants: Hardy, Yeats, Pound (in parts of "Mauberley"). Apart from a conceivably total lack of interest in war or a hatred of it, poets are not very likely to see wars in "peaceful" times (as if, worldwide, there were any such) as a fit subject for their attention. And yet here comes *Salient*, a remarkable work of poetry centering on probably the most terrible battle of WWI. It is known as "Third Ypres" (i.e., the third battle of Ypres in the entire war) since it took place in and around the Belgian town of that name, with especial stress on the last ridge east of Ypres: that muddy ocean of corpses, Passchendaele.

The author, Elizabeth Gray, is a woman with a multitude of talents. She has a B.A. with high honors from Radcliffe/Harvard and a J.D. with honors from Harvard Law School. She is an expert in complex negotiation and the formation and management of strategic alliances and other forms of interorganizational collaboration (of some utility one imagines in dealing with armies). She has lived and studied extensively in the Middle East and South Asia and has had long familiarity with Asian religions, especially Buddhism. Gray is a poet and a translator from classical Persian with distinguished work on Hafiz-i Shirazi and others of those great singers. More contemporaneously, she has worked with Iranian poets and musicians. To the point here, she is the author of a first book of poetry titled *Series | India*.

The latter collection is a very impressive and consistent work with its mixture of India herself, spirituality, and the personal. The entry through the Great Mother, the "Vulva of the Ten Worlds," into the savage beauty and immemorial violence of the subcontinent; the hard path to reaching and to recognizing India; the extensive work of *becoming* India (which is what the quest relates)—all of this travels in the head of anyone who has known and loved India and been set fire to, over and beyond its oceanic poverties, by its shattering beauty. Gray has a great gift of precision; every word tells ("a braid of words") and there are no weaknesses: the cloth (India is the great queen of the textile arts) is of one measure and of one piece:

But there must she thought, why we're, why
we seek the blue-milk sea, the crags of the mighty Vindhyas,
the Tower of the Ten Winds, the thread offered
that we can decline or use.

A great command of vocabulary; an uninterruptedly assured control of space on the page; a whole series of shortcuts to veracity ("Whether we are early or beauty," "Yes, absolutely you are from where," "We're going to myth her"); a masterly management of formidable myth; a constant tendency toward prose (a potential novel hides in the background) without ever departing from poetry ... and now, in not dissimilar terms, we reach *Salient*, a poem about a legendary WWI battle between Brits and Germans whose locus has earned it the title of "the Immortal Salient."

Throughout Gray's book, one is never at any remove from the facts and figures of the soldier's life, and one acquires, without huge technical headaches, a pertinent notion of the documentation. For example, one extraordinary work that Gray relies on is the vast *Artillery's Astrologers*, a 558-page "History of British Survey and Mapping on the Western Front 1914–1918" by Peter Chasseaud. A great deal of the closeness one develops to the individual combatants, to their movements on the ground, and to the groups into which they are divided, arises from Gray's disciplined and restrained use of this massive material. I'm reminded of sources for my own work in *Avia*, with sortie by sortie, battle by battle detail found, for instance, in the now classic works from a number of nations on the Battle of Britain in a subsequent war.

The achievement of *Salient* that strikes me first is the way collage succeeds every time, by its subtlety, its revelatory success while maintaining a profound simplicity. Gray has a sure hand in making poetry out of the most basic prose there can be: often the prose of military orders and reports. There is a constant occurrence of impromptu beauty, such as "color coming into the world"; "Eliminate those portions of this evidence which are obviously song"; the last lines of "Preliminary Orders," "as the flares and star shells do, / advance as light"; or the two-line poem, "This amulet protects the wearer against disappearing. // I place it in your hair." Everything invoked is crystal clear and yet retains its crystal mystery. There is a magical accession to the delineation of links and relationships that develop in the poem, even physical connections (real or imaginary) when moving from soldier to soldier, woman to soldier, poet to soldier, woman/poet to lover. There is a burning presence of absence, a constant coming and going between presence and absence: mainly the stress on the thousands of missing soldiers all the way through the poem until they achieve some kind of resurrection:

Some became smoke, cloud, and rain:

as when a pot breaks
the space within and the space without
become intermingled
                    the body reduced
to its atomic constituents indistinguishable
from the awareness within

Others dissolved into light from their feet upwards:

the heavy shelling at D.6.d.4.5
west of what remained of the church
for example
                    and after the light
faded from the sky there were no bodies

There is a constant struggle for vision: for *seeing* the war when so far from it: this is part of an ongoing conversation all through the work between visibility and occultation. Gray's use of quotes is vital to the poem, like this epigraph by Mark Larabee from his *Front Lines of Modernism*: "The continuing alteration of the ground makes it difficult to reconcile a vision of terrain at one point in time with its appearance in another.... This is not to say that under these circumstances one does not keep trying to see." And there is a full control of the arrival into the poem of the author, beginning physically early on with "Here I am straddling the Franco-Belgian frontier" and reaching full deployment in, say, "Where I stood watch, at your flank, alert, / behind the warm berm of your rib." While in "The Obstacle," the poet becomes most fully the soldier:

Then some kind of flare hovering
illuminating the daylight, filling the hollowed ground, then
implacable endurance, the residual
stubbornly held on to, history
again material, catching
at my clothes—some kind of affirmation—
until there it is, all of it—spider wire, snarls

of concertina, knife rests, chevaux-de-frise,
until the thing itself—as seen here

The "she," or "female," figure in the poem, when not the poet her-
self, appears to be a recurring Tantric Buddhist deity. For Elizabeth
can become the deity and the deity can become Elizabeth: this is
the formidable value of the occulted vestment in which the work is
clothed. At the outset, we must face the deployment of Buddhist Tan-
tra as a *co-primary* subject, as a repellent of the enemy (the German
army in this case) throughout the book to the very last passages. As to
the profundity of what it is that repels and that is repelled, virtually
not a word about who, or indeed, what is doing that. Tantra is a vast
realm: the part of it invoked here is primarily feminine and develops
the activity of female deities. These deities can be terrible in the toils
of this immense and terrifying war; they can also function as maternal
consolers and transformers of the terror and give meaning to what
appears totally meaningless. The immense *pardon* granted by and in-
herent in the visualizations of the maternal deities: to experience this
in the poem is to come naturally and simply upon the learning of an
answer—after centuries of the passing of such a multitude of lives.
Insofar as the Buddhist intention in almost any and all its chapters
is to *teach*, *Salient* has a message, however subtly and deeply, almost
invisibly, it is buried.

A poem as visionary and advisory as *Salient* in its return to a *reality*,
whatever time it belongs to, is what we look for in a *work*, knowing
that in the annals of worldwide suffering there is never truly any
peace at all. Here collage, as a massively omnipotent tactic, serves as
background, departs ... and poetry reenters: poetry as the rarest of
totalities. Yet it is able to leave room for the question of whether the
work has or has not a start and a finish, whether it is timed or timeless,
whether it is, or is not, an *ongoing* miraculous dialogue—again between
presence and absence.

For *Salient* we are deeply in debt to Elizabeth Gray.

—NATHANIEL TARN

## NOTES ON SOURCES

I cannot possibly list the array of materials that lie behind the almost three hundred poems from which these made the final cut. My intent here is to acknowledge those sources from which text has been imported directly, and to point the reader to related material that may be of interest.

### Maps

The primary resource for information on British survey and mapping in World War I is the work of Peter Chasseaud, particularly *Artillery's Astrologers: A History of British Survey and Mapping on the Western Front 1914–1918* (Lewes, East Sussex, U.K.: Mapbooks, 1999) and its companion volume *Topography of Armageddon: A British Trench Map Atlas of the Western Front 1914–1918*, also from Mapbooks, 1991.

The map of the British advance on p. 4 appears in *The Great World War: A History*, Vol. VII, edited by Frank A. Mumby and published in London by The Gresham Publishing Company Ltd. in 1919 (p. 247). Used with permission of Gresham Publishing.

The portion of British Trench Map M_90_000411.jpg that appears on p. 66, covering most of the Passchendaele battlefield and annotated by a Canadian unit, is used with the kind permission of the Imperial War Museum, London.

Digital versions of trench, artillery, administrative, and other kinds of military maps, as well as aerial photos, are widely available. I have found the Western Front Association's portfolio of DVDs most useful, primarily their two-disc set *Ypres: British Mapping 1914–1918*, which covers Square 28.

The geographical coordinates in the poems are identified using the trench map grid system developed by the Royal Survey Corps in 1914 and 1915 and used by the British throughout World War I. For the curious: http://www.greatwar.co.uk/research/maps/british-army-ww1-trench-maps.htm#findreference.

*Poems*

"War Magic" draws on *A History of How the Mongols Were Repelled* by Lodrö Gyaltsen (1552–1624), known simply as "Sokdokpa," in Jacob P. Dalton, *The Taming of the Demons: Violence and Liberation in Tibetan Buddhism* (New Haven, Connecticut: Yale University Press, 2011, 133–136). The shell numbers were found in Peter H. Liddle, *Passchendaele in Perspective: The Third Battle of Ypres* (Barnsley, South Yorkshire, U.K.: Leo Cooper, 1997). The Battle of the Somme was known to soldiers as "the Big Push"; the Battle of the Meuse-Argonne was known as "the Big Show"; the Schlieffen Plan was the battle plan developed in 1905 by Alfred Graf von Schlieffen, chief of the German General Staff at the time, that would enable Germany to fight a two-front war. It entailed a quick strike west through Belgium and the subsequent encirclement of Paris. As modified by Helmuth von Moltke, Schlieffen's successor, it formed the basis of the German assault against France and Belgium in August 1914.

"Taking Refuge" draws on *Machik's Complete Explanation: Clarifying the Meaning of Chöd*, translated by Sarah Harding (Ithaca, New York, and Boulder, Colorado: Tsadra Foundation, Snow Lion Publications, 2003, 142–144).

"In Some Ways the Situation Is Analogous to That Facing Second Army in 1915" draws on Chasseaud, *Artillery's Astrologers* (170).

"Recalling the *Bla*" draws on Samten G. Karmay, "The Soul and the Turquoise: A Ritual for Recalling the *Bla*," *The Arrow and the Spindle: Studies in History, Myths, Rituals and Beliefs in Tibet* (Kathmandu: Mandala Book Point, 1997, 314).

"The Missing" ("It was a test") is formally modeled after "Glyph" by Ann Lauterbach, *Under the Sign* (New York: Penguin, 2013). Lines in the poem draw from the following sources: *Ypres 1914: An Official Account Published by Order of the German General Staff*, translated by G. C. W. (London, 1919). *Machik's Complete Explanation*, 130–131. Alberto Ríos, "Some Thoughts on the Integrity of the Single Line in Poetry." Emily Rosko and Anton Vander Zee, Eds., *A Broken Thing: Poets on the Line* (Iowa City, Iowa: University of Iowa Press, 2011, 208–209).

"Indirect Fire: Shooting from the Map (from Appendix B)" draws on *Notes on Employment of Artillery in Trench Fighting* (Washington, D.C.: Army War College, May 1917, Sections 7 and 8); and from Chasseaud, *Artillery's Astrologers* (140). Section 11.0 includes a fragment of stanza four of Laurence Binyon's "For the Fallen."

"General Description of the Line" draws on "Notes for Infantry Officers on Trench Warfare," *British Trench Warfare 1917–1918: A Reference Manual*. General Staff, War Office. (London: The Imperial War Museum and Nashville, Tennessee: The Battery Press, 1997, 19–21).

"Bear in Mind" draws on handwritten annotations in the margins of a British trench map of the Auchy-Lens area in France, in Chasseaud's private collection, cited in *Artillery's Astrologers* (85, fn. 33). Geographical names and map coordinates have been altered to locate the poem in the Ypres Salient. This poem is dedicated to the Infantry Captain with the Cat, who taught me how to read it.

"How a Mark VII Trench Mortar Fuse Is Like Love" draws on *Handbook on Trench Mortar Fuzes: Mark VII and Mark VII-E* (Washington, D.C.: Ordnance Department, War Plans Division, War Department, April 1918, 10).

"Summary of Intelligence" draws on René de Nebesky-Wojkowitz, *Oracles and Demons of Tibet: The Cult and Iconography of the Tibetan Protective Deities* (The Hague: Mouton, 1956. Kathmandu and Varanasi: Book Faith India, 1993, 24–25).

"Additional Information" is for Elisabeth Lewis Corley.

"But You Knew This" draws from "Notes for Infantry Officers on Trench Warfare," *British Trench Warfare 1917–1918: A Reference Manual* (32–33).

"What She Told Me" (*"Girl, keep to these haunted places"*) draws on Dampa Sangye's prophecy delivered to Machik Lapdrön in *Machik's Complete Explanation* (67, fn. 297); see also Jerome Edou, *Machig Labdrön and the Foundations of Chöd* (Ithaca, New York: Snow Lion Publications, 1996, 131). The poem also draws on T. S. Eliot's "Little Gidding," Section I, lines 45–48, in *Four Quartets*. Wieltje Farm Cemetery is located in the center of a cornfield in the village of Sint-Jan, Ypres. It contains burials from July–October 1917, primarily the 2nd/4th Gloucesters.

"Notes on the Interpretation of Aeroplane Photographs" ("Examine the ground . . .") draws on *Notes and Illustrations on the Interpretation of Aeroplane Photographs. SS 550 and SS 550 A* (London: The War Office, March 1917. Brighton: FireStep Publishing and the National Army Museum, 2013, 5).

"Construction of Trench Systems: Explanation of Diagram #7" draws on *Notes on the Construction and Equipment of Trenches* (Washington, D.C.: Government Printing Office, 1917, 13).

"Amulet Against Madness" draws on Nik Douglas, *Tibetan Tantric*

*Charms and Amulets* (Mineola, New York: Dover Publications, 1978, Charm #127); and from Tadeusz Skorupski, *Tibetan Amulets* (Bangkok, Thailand: White Orchid Books, 1983, 41).

"Amulet Against Ground Deities" draws on Skorupski's *Tibetan Amulets* (41) and on *Gas Warfare. Part II. Methods of Defense Against Gas Attacks* (Washington, D.C.: U.S. Army War College, January 1918, 14–16).

"Chilled Feet" draws on *63rd (Royal Naval) Division Trench Standing Orders*, Second Edition (London: His Majesty's Stationery Office, 1917, Appendix III, 39).

"Actual Things with Characteristics" draws on *Machik's Complete Explanation* (121–122).

"The Obstacle" draws on *Manual of Field Works (All Arms). 1921. (Provisional.)* (London: His Majesty's Stationery Office, 1921, Sections 21–29, 17–58). Formally the poem owes a debt to "Thinking" by Jorie Graham, *The Errancy* (Hopewell, New Jersey: The Ecco Press, 1997, 40–41).

"Harm" draws on *Machik's Complete Explanation* (117–118).

"Preliminary Orders" draws on an image of the orders indicated in the title, found in Liddell, *Passchendaele in Perspective* (64).

"Inverted Maps" draws on Chasseaud, *Artillery's Astrologers* (54).

"She Explains How to Recognize the Signs of Specific Spirits and Demons When They Arise" draws on *Machik's Complete Explanation* (231, 240, 242–243).

"Near Wurst Farm" draws on *Machik's Complete Explanation* (101); and also Edou, *Machig Labdrön and the Foundations of Chöd* (163). The place called Wurst Farm by the British was located on trench map sheet 28 NE 1 Zonnebeke at D.7.d.9.9.

"Signatures" draws on *Manual of Field Works (All Arms). 1921. (Provisional.)* (93ff) and Terrence J. Finnegan, *Shooting the Front: Allied Aerial Reconnaissance in the First World War* (Stroud, Gloucestershire: The History Press, 2014, 182–208).

"Before the Attack on Poelcappelle" uses as background the actual meteorological forecasts issued in advance of the Battles of Broodseinde and Poelcappelle (multiple sources), and draws from the weather-makers section of de Nebesky-Wojkowitz, *Oracles and Demons of Tibet* (469–477).

"Obstacles" draws on *Manual of Field Works (All Arms). 1921. (Provisional.)* and from Patanjali's *Yoga Sutra*, II. 3–10.

"Amulet Against Dismemberment" is drawn from Collins, Major G.R.N., "Evacuation of the Sick and Wounded: Organization of Medical Units—System of Evacuation-Treatment-Invaliding-Red Cross Protection-Voluntary Organization." *Military Organization and Administration* (London: Hugh Rees Ltd., 1918. http://www.vlib.us/medical/evacn/evacn.htm).

"Sound Ranging" is a method of determining the geographical coordinates of a hostile artillery battery by using data received by microphones in multiple locations, each of which produces a bearing to the source of the sound. The poem draws on Chasseaud, *Artillery's Astrologers* (96–98), and on Sir Lawrence Bragg, Major-General A. H. Dowson, and Lieut.-Colonel H. H. Hemming, *Artillery Survey in the First World War* (London: Field Survey Association, 1971).

"Notes on the Interpretation of Aeroplane Photographs" ("Concentrate your whole mind") draws on *Notes and Illustrations on the Interpretation of Aeroplane Photographs* (5) and on *Machik's Complete Explanation* (188).

"The Guts of It" draws on a conversation recorded in Captain J. C. Dunn, *The War the Infantry Knew 1914–1919*, first published in 1938 (London: Abacus Books, 1994, 134). Captain Dunn was a Medical Officer of the Second Battalion, His Majesty's Twenty-Third Foot, The Royal Welsh Fusiliers, serving, for certain periods of the war, with Robert Graves and Siegfried Sassoon.

"In the Soft Parts of the Body" draws on Dr. Edmond Delorme, *Military Surgery* (London: H. K. Lewis, 1915, Chapter 10) and de Nebesky-Wojkowitz, *Oracles and Demons of Tibet* (365–368).

"Recognizing the Signs of Death" draws on Namchö Mingyur Dorje, *The Interpretation of Dreams in a 17th Century Tibetan Text*, translated by Enrico Dell'Angelo and Robin Cooke (Arcidosso, Italy: Shang Shung Edizioni, Associazione Culturale Comunita'Dzogchen, 1996, 14).

"The Relief" draws on Dunn, *The War the Infantry Knew* (159) and *Machik's Complete Explanation* (235).

"War Diary, 7th Infantry Brigade, 3rd Canadian Division" draws on the entries for 19–28 October 1917 in the daily unit War Diary of Princess Patricia's Canadian Light Infantry in the Canadian National Archives; also on Dalton, *Taming of the Demons* (130) and *Machik's Complete Explanation* (8).

"Instructions for Working with the *Gyalpo*" draws on *Machik's Complete Explanation* (233–234). The *gyalpo* (lit. "kings") are spirits that bring illness, impersonate leaders, and supposedly cause insanity.

"Further Instructions" draws on *Machik's Complete Explanation* (140–141).

"Telephone Reports: 2nd Canadian Divisional Artillery" draws on *Telephone Reports: 2nd Canadian Artillery, Zero Hour 6:00 a.m., 6 November 1917* (London: Imperial War Museum) and *Machik's Complete Explanation* (104–105, 110).

"The Missing: The Outer Signs" draws on Peter E. Hodgkinson, "Clearing the Dead" (http://www.vlib.us/wwi/resources/clearingthedead.html). After the Armistice, an organized attempt was made to clear the dead from the Flanders battlefields and to bring them to concentration cemeteries located nearby. Unidentified bodies are buried under a headstone that reads: "Here Lies a Soldier of the Great War, Known Unto God." The almost 90,000 names of those with no known grave can be found on the Menin Gate and Tyne Cot Memorials to the Missing.

"The Missing: The Secret Signs" draws on various Tibetan sources on the rainbow body quoted in Matthew T. Kapstein, "The Strange Death of Pema the Demon Tamer" in his edited volume *The Presence of Light: Divine Radiance and Religious Experience* (Chicago: The University of Chicago Press, 2004; 137, 141, 147).

"Field Survey": Hellfire Corner, at 28 NW 4 Ypres I.10.c.9.2, was a road and rail intersection critical for British troops and supply lines. German batteries in the surrounding hills had its location preregistered and shelled it constantly. The poem stole its last two lines from Ross White.

"The Missing" ("Some became smoke . . .") draws on various Tibetan sources in Kapstein, "The Strange Death of Pema the Demon Tamer" (137, 141, 147).

"Machik Lapdrön Tries to Explain One of the Immeasurables" draws on *Machik's Complete Explanation* (148–150).

"Given a Normally Fine August" draws on sections 55–61 of Sir Douglas Haig, *Dispatch #4 to the War Cabinet on the 1917 Campaigns in France and Belgium* (various sources).

"Camouflage: Trenches" draws on *Manual of Field Works (All Arms). 1921. (Provisional.)* (100).

"The Second Law of Occlusion" draws on *Notes on Map Reading for Use in Army Schools* (London: His Majesty's Stationery Office, 1915; 16, 19, 21).

"That One Time, in December 1914" refers to the Christmas Truce, which occurred in various sections of the line in France and Belgium on December 24–25, 1914. The poem draws on *Machik's Complete Explanation* (167–168).

"Our Bodies" draws on Sarah H. Jacoby, *Love and Liberation: Autobiographical Writings of the Tibetan Buddhist Visionary Sera Khandro* (New

York: Columbia University Press, 2014; 271, 296, 311) and C. G. Jung, *The Red Book: Liber Novus: A Reader's Edition*, edited by Sonu Shamdasani (New York: Philemon Foundation, W. W. Norton, 2009, 158).

"14 November 2017" draws on Dunn, *The War the Infantry Knew* (140–141).

"At Goudberg Copse" draws on *Machik's Complete Explanation* (163, 237) and John Jackson, *Private 12768: Memoir of a Tommy* (Stroud, Gloucestershire: The History Press, 2009; 94–96, 110). Jackson served in the 79th Regiment of Foot, The Queen's Own Cameron Highlanders, from 1914 until the Armistice. Jackson's text refers to High Wood, on the Somme, where the Camerons fought in 1916. I have taken the liberty of moving the location to the Ypres Salient, choosing equally deadly Goudberg Copse, located about 1,000 yards west of Vindictive Crossroads, at 20 SE 3 Westroosebeke V.29.b.1.1.

# ACKNOWLEDGMENTS

I am grateful to the editors of the following publications, in which sections of this work first appeared:

> *Little Star*, *Paris Lit Up* (Paris), *Ecotone*, *Bright Hill Press 25th Anniversary Anthology*, *Middlelost* (online), and *Cagibi* (online).

My primary debts of gratitude are reflected in the poem's dedication. I also want to express here my unbounded thanks to some of the many individuals who have offered insights, comments, and suggestions on this work as it evolved over time:

> to Elisabeth Lewis Corley and Joseph Megel at the University of North Carolina at Chapel Hill, for their development of the multimedia performance piece *Geomancy* in 2014; and also to the improvisational dance group AGA Collaborative, who co-created that work with them;

> to David Mahan at Yale Divinity School, and to Richard Deming, Nancy Kuhl, Henry Sussman, and others at the Yale Working Group on Contemporary Poetry and Poetics, for their meticulous attention to sacred landscape, contemporary poetry, and this piece of poetic work in particular;

> to Joseph Donahue and David Need at Duke University, and to Jessica Burstein at the University of Washington/Seattle, for their critical feedback and support;

> to the poets Maeve Kinkead, J. J. Penna, Alicia Jo Rabins, Maggie Schwed, and Abby Wender, who took the king's shilling and signed on with me for the duration of the War;

> to my Comrade-in-the-Military-Archives Nathaniel Tarn, whose *Avia*, surely in some way this poem's close cousin, I recently discovered;

to Paul Evans and Steve Hookins at the Royal Artillery Museum Archives in Woolwich, for their guidance in my search for original maps and materials (and for my special after-hours tour of the guns and their ghosts);

to the serving and retired military officers, British, Canadian, and American, whose responses to the poem have been illuminating and sustaining;

to my husband, Chip Loomis, and our sons, William and Sam, for their support (and patience) during my repeated absences in Flanders;

to the gracious, helpful, and understanding staff of the Ariane Hotel in Ieper/Ypres;

and to the numerous fellow Great War pilgrims I have met on the ground in Belgium, France, and the U.K.